THE CROSS

IN LIGHT OF THE WORK OF THE SOCIETY OF ST VINCENT DE PAUL

Fr Gerard Bogan

All booklets are published
thanks to the generosity of the supporters
of the Catholic Truth Society

Image Credits

Cover and the Stations: *Way of the Cross* in the Church of the Holy Trinity, Gemunden am, Germany | Shutterstock.com.
p5: *Frédéric Ozanam*, Wikimedia Commons (PD). p17: Pexel.com Shutterstock.com: p7: Jakub Krechowicz; p13: Srdjan Randjelovic; p21: Tverdokhlib; p25: wjarek; p29: Stephm2506; p33: Hamza Makhchoune; p37: hxdbzxy; p41: Roman Bodnarchuk; p45: Olga Pinegina; p49: estherpoon; p53: Mama Belle and the kids; p57: Jacob_09; p61: Matt Gush.

All rights reserved. First published 2023 by The Incorporated Catholic Truth Society, 42-46 Harleyford Road London SE11 5AY Tel: 020 7640 0042. Copyright © 2023 The Incorporated Catholic Truth Society. www.ctsbooks.org.

ISBN 978 1 78469 754 9

Contents

1st Station Jesus is condemned to death 7

2nd Station Jesus takes up his cross 11

3rd Station Jesus falls the first time................................. 15

4th Station Jesus meets his mother 19

5th Station Simon helps Jesus carry the cross 23

6th Station Veronica wipes the face of Jesus.................. 27

7th Station Jesus falls the second time 31

8th Station The Women of Jerusalem weep for Jesus.... 35

9th Station Jesus falls the third time................................ 39

10th Station Jesus is stripped of his garments................. 43

11th Station Jesus is nailed to the cross 47

12th Station Jesus dies on the cross 51

13th Station The body of Jesus is taken down from
the cross... 55

14th Station The body of Jesus is buried in the tomb...... 59

Frédéric Ozanam was the founder of the Society of St Vincent de Paul. While he was a student in Paris he gathered together a few friends with the aim of responding to the needs of the poor.

They decided that they would not promote any political viewpoint. Their motivation was to help people in need, regardless of who they were, or what they believed. If they were in need, then the society would respond to them. They placed their new society under the patronage of St Vincent de Paul.

This work is continued today, all over the world, by the sisters and brothers of the Society of St Vincent de Paul.

During this meditation on the Way of the Cross we will reflect on Jesus's way of suffering through the inspiration of Frédéric Ozanam and the society he founded to help the poor and those in need, the Society of St Vincent de Paul.

1ST STATION

1ST STATION
Jesus is condemned to death

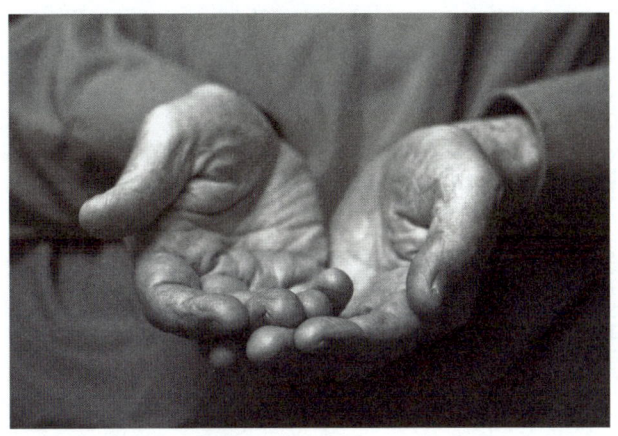

We adore you, O Christ, and we praise you.
Because by your Holy Cross you have redeemed the world.

Jesus stands before Pontius Pilate. Pilate thinks that he stands higher than Jesus, but this does not mean that he has right on his side. It only means that he has power. It is the power that has been given to him by his country's military occupation of another country. He feels uneasy before Jesus. Maybe Pilate knows that he is about to make a wrong decision. Perhaps, deep down inside himself, he has the sense that this moment is much bigger than two men facing each other. Pilate has power, nothing else.

Sometimes we are faced with unjust attacks. Often this is a case of someone with power wanting to exercise that power over us. Jesus, the Lord of Life, stood seemingly powerless before the might of the Roman army. 'You would have no power if it had not been given to you,' he said to Pilate. If we can unite our own suffering to the suffering of Jesus, then it may help us in our work with others in their suffering and powerlessness. When we can see our life as a gift from God it helps us to see that even our suffering can become sacred suffering. The prophet Isaiah: 'Ours were the sufferings he bore, ours the sorrows he carried.'

> *I love you Jesus*
> *my love above all things.*
> *I repent with my whole heart*
> *for having offended you.*
> *Never permit me*
> *to separate myself from you again.*
> *Grant that I may love you always*
> *and then do with me what you will.*
>
> *Holy Mother, pierce me through,*
> *in my heart each wound renew*
> *of my Saviour crucified.*

2ND STATION

2ND STATION
Jesus takes up his cross

We adore you, O Christ, and we praise you.
Because by your Holy Cross you have redeemed the world.

When Jesus takes up the cross it is the action of an innocent man who has been condemned to death. He had been betrayed and scourged. Now he was carrying the cross on which he would be brutally put to death. Even for a guilty person it would have been an unjust punishment. If someone is guilty of a crime, the State has the right to take away that person's liberty, their ability to move freely in society. The State, however, does not have the right to take away a person's dignity. This attack on Jesus was an assault on the human person.

At a meeting of the Society of St Vincent de Paul, its founder, Frédéric Ozanam, spoke of the political unrest under which France was living at the time. He highlighted the plight of thousands of poor people: in addition to the danger to life, because of political fighting, which they had to endure like everyone else, they also had the danger to life which came from their poverty. Frédéric declared that people were not created poor by God.[1] He criticised the parliament for not doing enough to respond to the situation.[2] In this way, Frédéric was issuing a call for social justice. But it was not a party-political statement. He was showing us it was as the Church that we needed to speak up for the poor.

> *I love you Jesus*
> *my love above all things.*
> *I repent with my whole heart*
> *for having offended you.*
> *Never permit me*
> *to separate myself from you again.*
> *Grant that I may love you always*
> *and then do with me what you will.*
>
> *Holy Mother, pierce me through,*
> *in my heart each wound renew*
> *of my Saviour crucified.*

3RD STATION

3ʳᴰ STATION

Jesus falls the first time

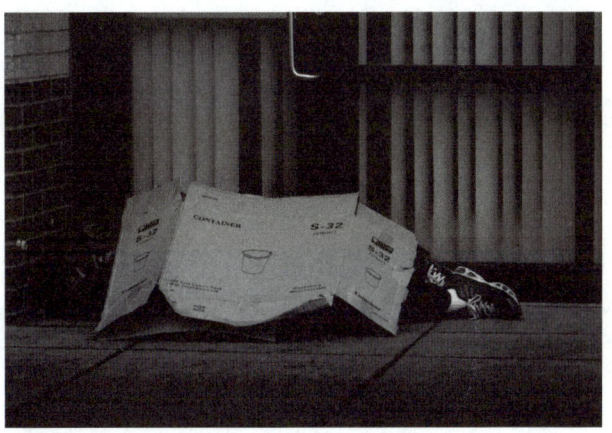

We adore you, O Christ, and we praise you.
Because by your Holy Cross you have redeemed the world.

Jesus had been weakened. Then he was forced to carry the heavy cross. It was too much for his frail human body. He fell. Even now, across the centuries, you can almost hear the wails let out by his family and his followers as his battered body hit the ground. They were beginning to feel the pain of Jesus. His pain was becoming their pain. They too had begun to walk the Sorrowful Way, the *Via Dolorosa*.

Frédéric did not want thanks for his help to those in need. For him, it was a privilege to do the work, and seeing first-hand the sufferings of the poor was a way to strengthen his own faith. Life had to be real. Indeed, he wrote that it would help the faith of many of his fellow Catholics if they had the opportunity to see the difficulties suffered by the poor. In this way their faith would stop being one bolstered by holy pictures: they would see the suffering Christ in the reality of the lives of the poor.[3]

> *I love you Jesus*
> *my love above all things.*
> *I repent with my whole heart*
> *for having offended you.*
> *Never permit me*
> *to separate myself from you again.*
> *Grant that I may love you always*
> *and then do with me what you will.*
>
> *Holy Mother, pierce me through,*
> *in my heart each wound renew*
> *of my Saviour crucified.*

4TH STATION

4TH STATION
Jesus meets his mother

We adore you, O Christ, and we praise you.
Because by your Holy Cross you have redeemed the world.

When the Angel Gabriel had asked Mary to be the mother of the Saviour, and she had said 'yes', she could not have imagined what she was now seeing before her eyes. The person who had been conceived out of perfect love was now being tortured by powerful men, men who were interested in their own desire for power, even at the expense of the human dignity and justice of other people.

Brother Roger of Taizé contends that one of the real obstacles to faith for some people is the idea of God as someone who judges us harshly;[4] and yet, St John tells us that God is love.[5] Brother Roger suggests that some Christians find it hard to believe that they are loved by God. It is almost as though they believe that God would love other people but not love them.[6]

I love you Jesus
my love above all things.
I repent with my whole heart
for having offended you.
Never permit me
to separate myself from you again.
Grant that I may love you always
and then do with me what you will.

Holy Mother, pierce me through,
in my heart each wound renew
of my Saviour crucified.

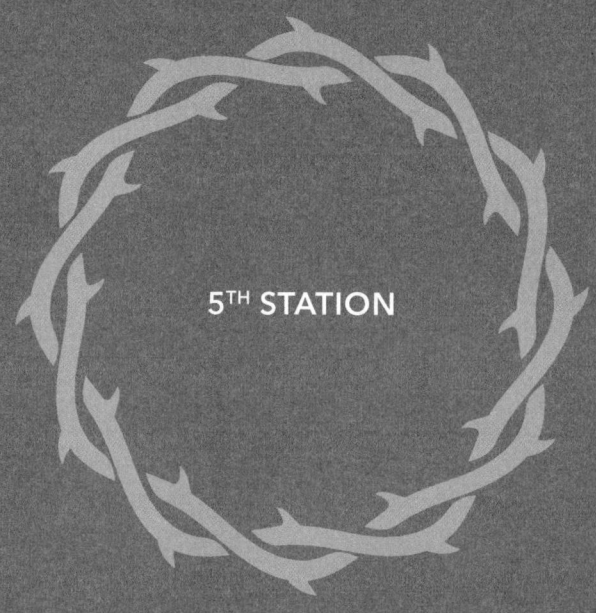

5TH STATION

5TH STATION
Simon helps Jesus carry the cross

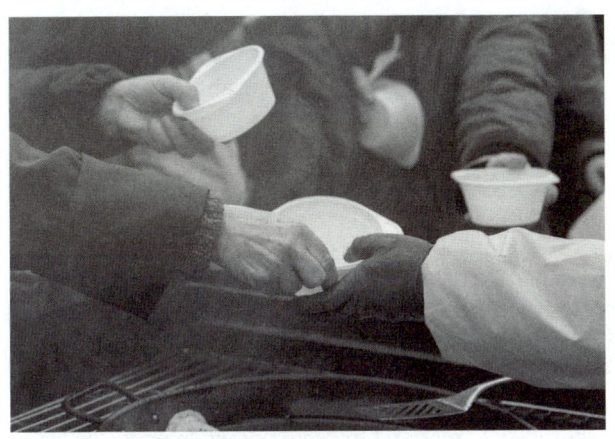

We adore you, O Christ, and we praise you.
Because by your Holy Cross you have redeemed the world.

What was Simon doing standing there? Had he been prevented from moving because of the big numbers of people squashed into narrow streets? Was he wondering what it was all about? Was he confused? Then they forced him to help Jesus carry the cross. Did he resent being made to do it? Or, was he frightened? We do not know the answers to these questions. But we do know that his sons, Alexander and Rufus, were members of the early Church.

Some of Frédéric's friends noticed Frédéric leaving the church after having attended Mass but not going straight home. They noticed that after Mass he would go to the baker's shop for bread which he then carried to the poor.[7] It was as if he were carrying the celebration of the Mass into the homes of the poor. When the followers of Jesus suggested that the crowds be sent away so that they could go and buy some food, Jesus told them to give them something themselves. They did not have enough. And yet, they found that when they started to distribute the bread there was enough for everyone. Frédéric Ozanam knew that the work of the Society of St Vincent de Paul, and of all members of the Church, is to respond to every person in need.

I love you Jesus
my love above all things.
I repent with my whole heart
for having offended you.
Never permit me
to separate myself from you again.
Grant that I may love you always
and then do with me what you will.

Holy Mother, pierce me through,
in my heart each wound renew
of my Saviour crucified.

6TH STATION

6TH STATION

Veronica wipes the face of Jesus

We adore you, O Christ, and we praise you.
Because by your Holy Cross you have redeemed the world.

The person of Veronica is not mentioned in the Scriptures. She is a product of Christian tradition, but that does not make her any less real. Moved with pity for Jesus, we are told that she wiped his face with a cloth and the imprint of Jesus's face remained on the cloth. Fittingly, the name tradition gives this woman, 'Veronica', means true image, true icon.

Whenever we are able to respond to each other in love, we are responding to Jesus. When we feed the hungry, it is Jesus we are feeding. When we clothe the naked, it is Jesus we are clothing. When we share a smile, or a conversation, or listen with attentiveness, we are doing this to Jesus. In this way our work becomes his work. Our thoughts are his thoughts. Our life becomes his life.[8]

> *I love you Jesus*
> *my love above all things.*
> *I repent with my whole heart*
> *for having offended you.*
> *Never permit me*
> *to separate myself from you again.*
> *Grant that I may love you always*
> *and then do with me what you will.*
>
> *Holy Mother, pierce me through,*
> *in my heart each wound renew*
> *of my Saviour crucified.*

7ᵀᴴ STATION

7TH STATION
Jesus falls the second time

We adore you, O Christ, and we praise you.
Because by your Holy Cross you have redeemed the world.

Even with Simon helping him, Jesus falls a second time under the weight of the cross. It is the weight not only of wood, but of the sins of humanity. He is carrying those sins with him. The One who is without sin is bearing in his own body the sins of all of us. He is carrying them so that he might free us from any power we think they may have over us.

St Teresa of Calcutta teaches us that it is when we act in charity towards the poor that we are loving Jesus. The mystery of the Incarnation, God becoming a human person in Jesus, does not make sense if we limit it to the person of Jesus. Therefore, the challenge for all Christians is to show how this Incarnation can be seen in the life of every human person. If we want to look for God in our lives, we should look, St Teresa tells us, to the lives of the poor.

> *I love you Jesus*
> *my love above all things.*
> *I repent with my whole heart*
> *for having offended you.*
> *Never permit me*
> *to separate myself from you again.*
> *Grant that I may love you always*
> *and then do with me what you will.*
>
> *Holy Mother, pierce me through,*
> *in my heart each wound renew*
> *of my Saviour crucified.*

8TH STATION

8TH STATION

The Women of Jerusalem weep for Jesus

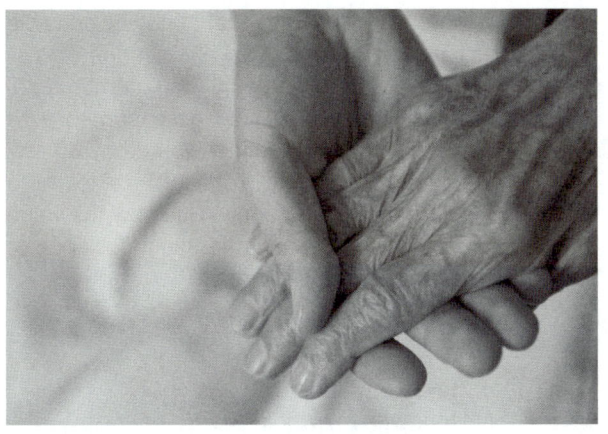

We adore you, O Christ, and we praise you.
Because by your Holy Cross you have redeemed the world.

'Daughters of Jerusalem, weep not for me but for yourselves and your children.' This most memorable line shows us that the real sorrow of the situation is not simply what the powerful have done to Jesus, but what human beings are capable of doing to each other. If we are to attempt to understand the person of Jesus, we have to try to appreciate what it means to be human.

Brother Roger of Taizé writes that it may be possible to consider listening to others as a vocation.[9] This is one of the things that St Vincent de Paul members do. There are times when people just need someone to listen to them. In this way they feel wanted by others. One of the things which Brother Roger of Taizé learnt to do was to listen carefully to people. He knew the value of listening and he also appreciated the importance of feeling that someone was prepared to listen to you.

> *I love you Jesus*
> *my love above all things.*
> *I repent with my whole heart*
> *for having offended you.*
> *Never permit me*
> *to separate myself from you again.*
> *Grant that I may love you always*
> *and then do with me what you will.*
>
> *Holy Mother, pierce me through,*
> *in my heart each wound renew*
> *of my Saviour crucified.*

9TH STATION

9TH STATION
Jesus falls the third time

We adore you, O Christ, and we praise you.
Because by your Holy Cross you have redeemed the world.

Does this third fall of Jesus remind us that Peter denied Jesus three times? Would Peter have been aware of that? After the Resurrection Jesus asked Peter three times if he loved him, and three times he answered that he did love him. What matters is not the number of times we fall into sin; what matters is the number of times we lovingly return to Jesus.

Frédéric Ozanam understood that the life of faith involved both prayer and good works. Some people will devote themselves more to one area than another, but it is for all Christians to be involved to some extent with both.

> *I love you Jesus*
> *my love above all things.*
> *I repent with my whole heart*
> *for having offended you.*
> *Never permit me*
> *to separate myself from you again.*
> *Grant that I may love you always*
> *and then do with me what you will.*
>
> *Holy Mother, pierce me through,*
> *in my heart each wound renew*
> *of my Saviour crucified.*

10TH STATION

10ᵀᴴ STATION
Jesus is stripped of his garments

We adore you, O Christ, and we praise you.
Because by your Holy Cross you have redeemed the world.

This is an act of humiliation. Not satisfied with the torture they had inflicted upon Jesus, they also humiliated him. Any act of humiliating another human being is wrong. No matter the situation, there is never an excuse for it. It is an attack on their true dignity; it is an attack on the human person who has been made in the image and likeness of God.

Frédéric Ozanam, the founder of the Society of St Vincent de Paul, was a man deeply committed to his Catholic Faith. He knew that living the Faith could not be reduced to a few prayers. It meant, for him, the total commitment of his life to God — in his prayer, through his family, through his help for the poor.

> *I love you Jesus*
> *my love above all things.*
> *I repent with my whole heart*
> *for having offended you.*
> *Never permit me*
> *to separate myself from you again.*
> *Grant that I may love you always*
> *and then do with me what you will.*
>
> *Holy Mother, pierce me through,*
> *in my heart each wound renew*
> *of my Saviour crucified.*

11TH STATION

11th STATION

Jesus is nailed to the cross

We adore you, O Christ, and we praise you.
Because by your Holy Cross you have redeemed the world.

This was extreme brutality. To hammer large, rough nails into the body of a human being is an act of barbarism. Every hammer blow is an assault on the person of Jesus, but also on humanity itself. Such cruelty causes intense suffering. It also injures the humanity of the person who is inflicting the suffering. Cruelty is not worthy of the human condition.

Frédéric Ozanam felt that in his time there were increasing tensions between the rich and the poor. He also recognised that among the members of the St Vincent de Paul conferences there was a real feeling of happiness. This pleased him, and it also encouraged him to believe that his brothers might be the very group who could do something about the lack of harmony between the rich and poor. The teaching of the Church, to which he faithfully adhered, was that all people had been created in the image and likeness of God.

> *I love you Jesus*
> *my love above all things.*
> *I repent with my whole heart*
> *for having offended you.*
> *Never permit me*
> *to separate myself from you again.*
> *Grant that I may love you always*
> *and then do with me what you will.*
>
> *Holy Mother, pierce me through,*
> *in my heart each wound renew*
> *of my Saviour crucified.*

12TH STATION

12TH STATION

Jesus dies on the cross

We adore you, O Christ, and we praise you.
Because by your Holy Cross you have redeemed the world.

Under the cross stood his mother, Mary, some other women, and St John. This was suffering with the suffering Jesus. It was sharing his pain and his anguish.

For St Teresa of Calcutta the words of Jesus on the cross, 'I thirst', are also the cry of the poor. It is the cry of all who are thirsting for water, but also for food, and for life itself. It is the cry of those who want to be treated with the dignity that belongs to every human person.

> *I love you Jesus*
> *my love above all things.*
> *I repent with my whole heart*
> *for having offended you.*
> *Never permit me*
> *to separate myself from you again.*
> *Grant that I may love you always*
> *and then do with me what you will.*
>
> *Holy Mother, pierce me through,*
> *in my heart each wound renew*
> *of my Saviour crucified.*

13TH STATION

13TH STATION
The body of Jesus is taken down from the cross

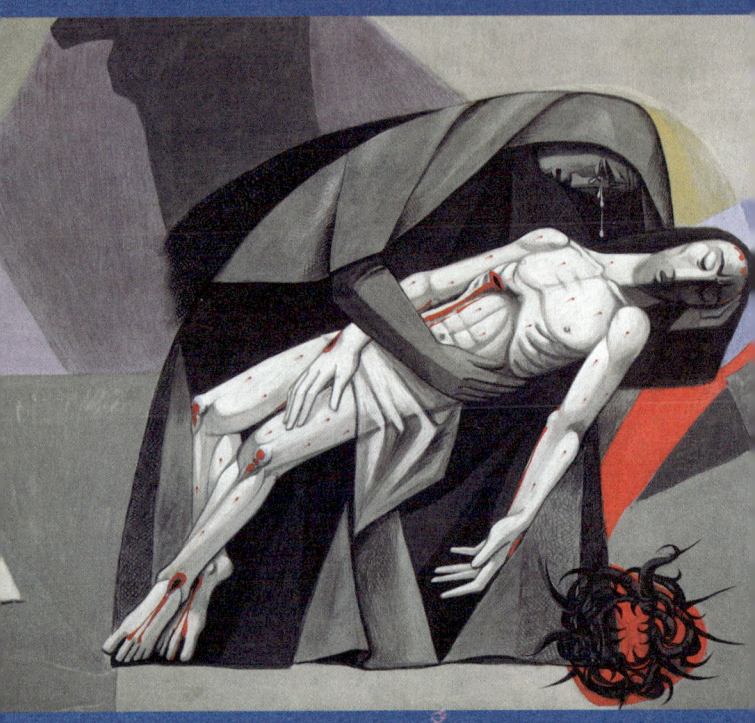

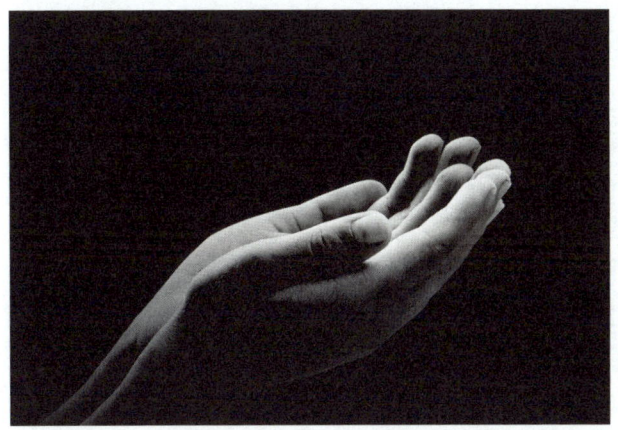

We adore you, O Christ, and we praise you.
Because by your Holy Cross you have redeemed the world.

Mary holds the body of the dead Jesus. When the Angel Gabriel had asked her to be the mother of the Saviour she had trusted that God's will would be done. Even now, at this moment of sheer desolation, she trusted that God's will would be done. She did not know how.

If Christians are going to be people who will work for the proclamation of the Gospel we need to be people of prayer. Brother Roger of Taizé writes that often young people will tell him that they do not know how to pray. His reply is that even the desire for prayer can be the start of prayer itself. It can be the beginning of a life with God which grows into our being aware of coming very close to him.[10] Sometimes this will mean that the person has a sense of God's presence, even if they are not sure how to talk about it. But it is also important to remember that God is with us whether we feel his presence or not.

> *I love you Jesus*
> *my love above all things.*
> *I repent with my whole heart*
> *for having offended you.*
> *Never permit me*
> *to separate myself from you again.*
> *Grant that I may love you always*
> *and then do with me what you will.*
>
> *Holy Mother, pierce me through,*
> *in my heart each wound renew*
> *of my Saviour crucified.*

14TH STATION

14TH STATION

The body of Jesus is buried in the tomb

We adore you, O Christ, and we praise you.
Because by your Holy Cross you have redeemed the world.

The body of the dead Jesus was placed in the tomb. The stone closed the entrance. It seemed so final. But death does not have the last word. Death could not hold the Lord of Life.

Frédéric Ozanam knew that what mattered for Christians was the twofold apostolate of faith and charity: the two great commandments of Jesus to love God and our neighbour. Ozanam called upon all people to re-learn the maxims of the Gospel and to practise them in justice and charity that would permeate their lives and the social institutions around them. In his lecture hall, at his desk and in the slums, he spread the truth, followed in the footsteps of Christ, and urged his companions to give themselves generously to God and their neighbour.

> *I love you Jesus*
> *my love above all things.*
> *I repent with my whole heart*
> *for having offended you.*
> *Never permit me*
> *to separate myself from you again.*
> *Grant that I may love you always*
> *and then do with me what you will.*
>
> *Holy Mother, pierce me through,*
> *in my heart each wound renew*
> *of my Saviour crucified.*

Prayers for Our Holy Father, the Pope

Our Father…, Hail Mary…, Glory Be…

Endnotes

1. James Patrick Derum, *Apostle in a Top Hat* (St Louis, Missouri: Society of St Vincent de Paul, Council of the United States, 1995) 217.

2. Ibid.

3. 'Letter to Fr Pendola, 19th July 1853', quoted in Austin Fagan, *Through the Eye of a Needle* (Middlegreen, Slough: St Paul Publications, 1989) 203.

4. Brother Roger of Taizé, 'Let the simple heart rejoice!', Mother Teresa & Brother Roger, *Prayer, Seeking the Heart of God* (London: Harper Collins Publishers, 1992) 28-9.

5. *1 Jn* 4.8, *et passim*.

6. Brother Roger of Taizé, 'Let the simple heart rejoice!' (1992) 28-9.

7. Kathleen O'Meara, *Frederic Ozanam: Professor at the Sorbonne, His Life and Works* (London: C. Kegan Paul & Co., 2nd edition, 1878; repr. London: Forgotten Books, 2017) 238.

8. St Teresa of Calcutta, 'To serve the poor', Mother Teresa & Brother Roger, *Prayer, Seeking the Heart of God* (London: Harper Collins Publishers, 1992) 84.

9. *Choose to Love*, Brother Roger of Taizé 1915-2005 (Taizé: Ateliers et Presse de Taizé, 2007) 62-3.

10. Ibid. 58-9.